THE
MASTERPIECE
MINDSET

CARLETTE BRADLEY

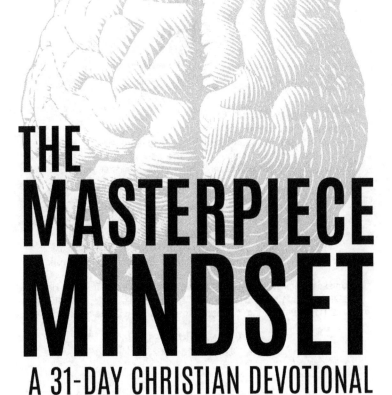

THE MASTERPIECE MINDSET

A 31-DAY CHRISTIAN DEVOTIONAL
WRITTEN TO HELP ANYONE EXPERIENCING A GREAT LOSS OR A TRANSFORMATIONAL TIME IN THEIR LIFE

XULON PRESS

Xulon Press
2301 Lucien Way #415
Maitland, FL 32751
407.339.4217
www.xulonpress.com

Paperback ISBN-13: 978-1-6628-4010-4
Ebook ISBN-13: 978-1-6628-4011-1

||||||||||||||||||||||||||||||||||||||||||||||||||||||||||||||||||||||||||||||||||||||||||||||

This devotional is dedicated to my beloved
daughter, Dierra. Without you, I am
certain that many days I would not have a
reason to live. You are my muse. I love you.

||||||||||||||||||||||||||||||||||||||||||||||||||||||||||||||||||||||||||||||||||||||||||||||

||||||||||||||||||||||||||||||||||||||||||||||||||||||||||||||||||||||||||||||||||||||||||||||

A special thank you to Kenyetta Moore.
Girl, you are a true gem.

||||||||||||||||||||||||||||||||||||||||||||||||||||||||||||||||||||||||||||||||||||||||||||||

Why a Masterpiece Mindset? Well, simply because it is my divine purpose to help everyone that I encounter believe that they are masterpieces according to the scripture Ephesians 2:10 NLT. When we truly believe that we are God's design, his handiwork, his divine creation, we can find the courage to align our lives accordingly. Everything that we do and yes, everything that we think should demonstrate our belief system. Our minds belong to God. A mindset is a set of beliefs that dictate our behaviors and our decisions. Having a Godly mindset means that we have a Masterpiece Mindset. I pray that your spirit will leap as these words from my heart penetrate through your pain or experience. Be blessed my brothers and my sisters.

Introduction:

The key to having the right mindset in the midst of great loss, or any great transition in your life, begins with having the right perspective of who God is.

Perhaps you are (experiencing) in the midst of a transition right now, or (still) healing from an aged loss that feels just as fresh as yesterday.

This devotional is designed to help you discover and apply; kingdom practices (perspectives and processes) to promote a Christ mindset, wherever you are in your healing process.

It is important to be aware that the adversary wants to steal, kill, and destroy, our minds and our relationship with God, one way is through sorrow. But God is close to the broken hearted.

I am no stranger to this life after loss process. As I journey to write this universal help guide, a short three weeks and three days after my beloved husband Antwain passed away, unexpectedly, I hope to help myself and others walk through this valley of Loss.

My world has been completely turned upside down, and my heart has a gaping hole in it. My home is empty, my nights are sleepless, and every day I think I encounter a different emotion. Some emotions I can identify, others I cannot. Everything is just so raw, like an open sore. I miss him so much and what used to feel partially certain, is anybody's guess. I don't understand why this happened. I may never understand why this happened. Yet I know that God loves me.

I also know that loss does not stop my journey in the Lord. I must continue to trust God with everything that I have. To lean in to my internal knowing of who HE is. It's the knowing that pushes me daily to actively take every thought captive that wants to exalt itself above who I know God to be.

I face each day refusing to lay down and die. I actively decide that each and every anti-God thought has to go. I refuse to be consumed or in a sunken place of emotions. God doesn't want that for me, and I know that my husband wouldn't want that for me either. I stand on the truth that, if I am not dead then God is not done with me yet. Friends, if WE are not dead, then God is not done with US yet!

As you get through this devotional. I encourage you to have journal nearby. Write down the thoughts that are trying to consume you (this will be a living document as thoughts change daily). Commit to confessing each thought that wants to hold you captive. Pause where you are right now and give those thoughts to the Lord, He is the only one that can handle them.

||||||||||||||||||||||||||||||||||||||||||||||||||||||||||||||||||||||||||||||||||||||||||||||||||||||||||||

2 Corinthians 2:5 We demolish arguments and every pretension that sets itself up against the knowledge of God, and we take captive every thought to make it obedient to Christ.

||||||||||||||||||||||||||||||||||||||||||||||||||||||||||||||||||||||||||||||||||||||||||||||||||||||||||||

Day 1

For the 1st week or so after Antwain's death, I kept having flashbacks of the EMTs performing CPR on him. I wanted that vision erased from my memory because his life was too beautiful, too impactful to be summed up by his death.

Each time the vision would pop into my mind, I would whisper "Lord, please take this away".

It was still so fresh, so cutting. I could still feel my stomach drop every time his body flinched at the chest compressions. A scene that seemed too vivid to just be a horrific memory.

An acquaintance, who happens to be a widow suggested that I pray differently when these visions arise. So, I asked God to replace the visions of loss with visions of what God wanted me to see. One evening as I prayed that prayer and laid down on the couch, I looked up and the reflection of the sunset was shining through my blinds, peering through the large picture window.

What I saw were images of crosses being created through the sunset light. There were about seven of them. When it occurred to me what I was looking at, all I could do was laugh.

God is amazing and uses the simplest things to create life changing moments in our lives. *"God moments"* are what I call them. How does this experience affect my mindset? It's a reminder and motivator, to first continue to confess my feelings honestly to God as often as I have them. Second, to focus on the promises of God because what Jesus did on Calvary for all of us is enough confirmation that He's not going to leave you, nor I alone buried in our troubles.

Take Action: Check to see if you are paying attention to the small things that God is sending along the way to answer your prayer. You could be overlooking them because the pain is great. When the pain is great, it's hard to take your mind off it. It's raw, it is agonizing, and unbearable at times. The good news is that Jesus knows that pain. Try to focus on that truth.

What painful images are nagging your spirit? Write them down. Confess them. Ask God to remove them and replace them. (You have to want to let them go in order to release them fully.)

||||||||||||||||||||||||||||||||||||||||||||||||||||||||||||||||||||||||||||||||||||||||||||||||

Psalm 34:18 The LORD is near to the brokenhearted and saves the crushed in spirit.

||||||||||||||||||||||||||||||||||||||||||||||||||||||||||||||||||||||||||||||||||||||||||||||||

NOTES:

_____

_____

_____

_____

_____

_____

_____

Day 2

Today I want to focus on gratitude. Counting blessings instead of focusing on my pain brings me rest and reminds me that God is worthy, no matter the loss HE is a giver. It's important to acknowledge God, not only for what HE is currently doing, but for the things HE has already done. How has HE blessed you over the years and how has HE been an ever-present help throughout your life? Personally, I am so eternally grateful for the love that Antwain and I shared. It was deep. It was intense. It was forgiving and it was transformational. I am so grateful for all the beautiful memories, they keep me. My husband and I experienced many "firsts" together and we were intentional about being mindful of those moments. I'm grateful. Grateful for all the times that he made me so angry that I wanted to spit nails into the wall, I'm grateful. Those times taught me so much about myself. I gained so much strength, courage and wisdom being his wife. I'm grateful that I learned how to love despite how I felt at times. After every disagreement we would say, "it doesn't change how I feel about you". We never left the knowing of our love for one another to chance or guess, we were both very certain. I'm grateful for all the songs we sang together. All the dances we danced together. Every sunset we watched, tears we cried and laughs we laughed. Such an enormous bundle of yes! Yes Father, I am ever grateful.

Take Action: I implore you to find the time and value of counting your blessings, whatever situation you're in. The recollection of God's goodness will change your perspective and certainly put a smile on your face. If you really dig deep, it'll send you right into a praise break! God is just that good! I vow to always have a memorial in my heart for the goodness of the Lord in my marriage. To God be the glory!

What blessings come to mind when you think of the goodness of God? It's not always tangible, but it is the internal blessings that have meant so much to me during this time. Can you focus on having more gratitude instead of holding yourself hostage by counting your losses? Where do your thoughts go when you think about telling God thank you? When was the last time your prayer was only full of thankfulness?

||||||||||||||||||||||||||||||||||||||||||||||||||||||||||||||||||||||||||||||||||||||||||||||||||||||||||

1 **Thessalonians 5:18 give thanks in all circumstances; for this is God's will for you in Christ Jesus.**

||||||||||||||||||||||||||||||||||||||||||||||||||||||||||||||||||||||||||||||||||||||||||||||||||||||||||

NOTES:

_____

_____

_____

_____

_____

_____

_____

Day 3

Today marks four long weeks since my sweetheart left this earth. It's Friday, and every Friday since has been really rough for me emotionally. I used to look forward to Fridays like most working adults, but now not so much. I know that this is still the day that the Lord has made, and I want to rejoice and be glad in it. But If I'm being honest, it's rough out here for a sister to rejoice. Yet because of my internal knowing, I'm seeking HIM to teach me how, to not just live or survive, but rejoice! As Fridays are obviously a regular part of the weekly calendar, 52 a year, for however long the Lord sees fit. I do not intend to surrender Fridays to depression and sadness. I am certainly grateful to know that God knows exactly how I feel and as the tears flow, I will continue to confess my feelings to HIM. I also understand that rejoicing and being glad doesn't necessarily mean that I should be jumping up and down, but I believe if the language of my heart and prayers is giving God glory internally then that will eventually lead me to having Fridays that are full of external joy as well. This time in my life seems to be the toughest that I have ever had. So, I ask myself how can I dig a little deeper to rejoice and be glad on Fridays and every day?

True joy is never dependent upon circumstance. For me, my joy is based on my relationship with my heavenly Father. So even though I'm hurting, I still have joy. It's mine. I took ownership of it when I said yes to Jesus. Think of all the worldly possessions we own. Just because we don't use them every day doesn't mean that we've lost ownership. We choose everyday which possessions to use. I have to choose joy. I have to make a decision. Even if that decision comes after an hour of crying and an hour-long pity party. I have to make a decision. A decision is easier to make when you have all the facts. What facts do I know for certain? God is good. His love endures forever. God is faithful to help me when I ask. HE is the only one that can mend my broken heart. God answers prayer. God is perfect. There are endless facts about God that I personally know to be true. If I choose to focus on those facts on Fridays and every day, then I believe that the joy of the Lord will be my strength. I've made my decision to rejoice and be glad in it, because I am alive, and I still have purpose!

Take Action: How do you measure success? How do you define joy? Is your joy easily stolen or do you easily give it away? How can you begin to take back ownership of the joy of the Lord that is your strength?

|||||||||||||||||||||||||||||||||||||||||||||||||||||||||||||||||||||||||||||||||||||||||||||||

Psalm 118:24 The Lord has done it this very day; let us rejoice toDay and be glad.

|||||||||||||||||||||||||||||||||||||||||||||||||||||||||||||||||||||||||||||||||||||||||||||||

NOTES:

_____

_____

_____

_____

_____

_____

Day 4

Today is a day of scattered rain showers. Over the years I have come to love the rain, especially the smell of it. There are times that my husband would literally sit or dance in the rain. He absolutely loved the rain. Our shared love for the rain now has a bit of new meaning for me. As I sit here on the corner of the couch with the front door open just enough for me to glare at the raindrops as they fall, my hope is being renewed. My tears and unpredictable moments of grief can be compared to the rain. Some days they have been scattered, some days thunderous and scary and even unexpected, but to my surprise they pass over. Rain is necessary. My tears are necessary.

I find great comfort in knowing that God collects my tears according to Psalms 56:8-9. The rain clears the air, allows plants to grow and aids to continue the cycle of life. It is more than just coincidence that tears have some of the same benefits. I won't fight the tears when they want to fall. I'm going to ride these waves of grief as if I was an award-winning surfer. I will welcome my tears to bring healing, spiritual cleansing, and a harvest of joy. They will allow every seed I plant in my prayers according to God's will to grow and manifest themselves. Finally, I will allow my tears to produce natural and spiritual growth while I purposefully live out the cycle of life that God has predestined for me long ago.

Take Action: When your tears want to fall, do you fight them? How can you begin to connect your tears to healing and spiritual growth? List the benefits of your tears.

I declare that my tears will _____

_____ .

||||||||||||||||||||||||||||||||||||||||||||||||||||||||||||||||||||||||||||||||||||||||||||||||||||||||

Psalm 56:8 Record my misery; list my tears on your scroll, are they not in your record?

||||||||||||||||||||||||||||||||||||||||||||||||||||||||||||||||||||||||||||||||||||||||||||||||||||||||

NOTES:

_____

_____

_____

_____

_____

_____

_____

_____

Day 5

In this morning's vision of the day my husband passed away, I could hear a bit of audio. I recall the tone that I was taking with God, as an officer and my cousin held me back from getting close to his lifeless body, as he lay on the ground. I don't believe I've ever taken a stern almost angry tone with God ever in my life before this day. "No, God, No! God please don't take him now! God, no, no, no, no, NO! Please don't do this to me!" As I was on my way to the hospital to meet the ambulance, my stern pleading continued in the car. "God, I know that this is NOT happening. I am loyal! I do what You tell me to do! Please revive my husband NOW!" That tone came from a deep place of pain, hurt, broken expectation and frankly entitlement. At that moment, I thought that I was entitled to what I imagined as the perfect healing or miracle. That the physicality of our love story was not to end, in this moment, at this time, on this day.

That tone didn't last long. Once my husband was pronounced, shock took over, and then, I began to worship God right there where I stood. My voice was very faint and I'm not sure if anyone else could hear me, but my worship was a confession and an act of trust. I lost my husband and chose in this moment to worship my first Husband, according to Isaiah 54:5 "For your Creator is your husband the Lord God is His name." Antwain was gone, God remained.

What do you do when God doesn't answer your prayer? Let go of what you don't understand. Understanding will fail you but putting your trust in God will keep you close to Him. It doesn't happen overnight, but it will happen. You will see His goodness again. Trust brings peace and peace is our greatest need. Jesus left us with perfect peace. Something will be birthed out of the brokenness and pain. You will have hope again. In the moment, you feel like you are in a dark valley of despair, but the light is always there, you just have to look for it.

Take Action: What do you need to do to let go of trying to understand? Is it time to stop asking why you had to go through something? Why not you? How can you affirm your trust in God over what you feel? What characteristic is God developing in you that outweighs hopelessness?

Philippians 4:6-7 Do not be anxious about anything, but in every situation, by prayer and petition, with thanksgiving, present your requests to God. 7 And the peace of God, which transcends all understanding, will guard your hearts and your minds in Christ Jesus.

NOTES:

_____

_____

_____

_____

_____

_____

Day 6

Oh Lord, the sound of my cry in this season! The piercing screams that I let out from time to time, along with the deep baritone sulking that escapes from my voice box are sounds that I've never heard before. Some of the time I look around to see if it's really me. I know, it sounds silly but I'm just telling the truth. In those moments I truly have no words and all I can do is go through the moment and allow myself to be mindful of the moment and that I'll come out of it, in time. It's over when it's over. I can closely relate to the story of Hannah in 1 Samuel chapter 1 when she was crying out, lips moving with no sound. The priest thought that she was drunk. I can understand how emotional pain can be confused with drunkenness. God hears my cries of distress, and He will answer them. I have confidence in that. My cry, whether it has a lack of sound, or the times when my cry stretches itself into its many sounds, pitches, and depths, will rise to God, and because Jesus wept, I know that He understands, and He cares.

Over the years, I used to believe that crying was a sign of weakness, but I now know that my tears are a symbol of strength. Not my own strength, but the strength of God and in His spirit that comforts me and intercedes for me when I can do nothing but moan. My grief will turn to joy, and I trust that joy comes in the morning. My morning is determined by God's timing and not my own. I find comfort in meditating on John 16:20, God has the power, mercy, and grace to turn my grief to joy. I have the power to surrender.

Take Action: Have you believed that your tears are a sign of weakness? What can you do to fortify your belief that God receives your tears and will use them for your benefit? Have you held back tears that have promoted other issues such as migraines, illness, anger, restlessness, faithlessness, etc.?

||||||||||||||||||||||||||||||||||||||||||||||||||||||||||||||||||||||||||||||||||||||||||||||||||||||||||

John 16:20 very truly I tell you, you will weep and mourn while the world rejoices. You will grieve, but your grief will turn to joy.

||||||||||||||||||||||||||||||||||||||||||||||||||||||||||||||||||||||||||||||||||||||||||||||||||||||||||

NOTES:

_____

_____

_____

_____

_____

_____

_____

Day 7

Such a bittersweet morning to return to work, after two months away from my career. However, you define the time; "sixty days", "eight weeks", "beginning of a new quarter" this first day back reminds me that there are still many "firsts without him" to experience. There was the first night I slept alone, the first meal I was actually able to eat, the first morning without a kiss, the first story I couldn't share, and now I am heading back to work without Antwain sending me off to conquer the world. I am feeling all sorts of emotions today. I have cried several times without warning. I am also full of gratitude, but I must say, I miss my life partner terribly. Through the crushing, I was reminded in prayer of the powerful right hand of our heavenly Father. I don't know about any of you, but I was a Daddy's girl and if I ever fell off my bike or experienced any other pain that required relief, I would reach for my Daddy's right hand. His hand brought sustaining comfort and assurance that I wasn't alone, that I was protected. In this process I still have a Daddy and I call him ABBA. His right hand provides me with strength, ability, protection, salvation, promise, provision, and so much more. Think of how many times we see God's right hand mentioned in the bible. It's clearly something that we should be aware of and all its majestic power and shattering strength! Today I am depending upon the right hand of ABBA Daddy God, to pull me out of where I don't belong. To set me where He wants me to be, and to give me the footing that I need. HIS right hand will remove fear, apprehension, and give me the courage to live now. I expect HIS right hand to provide relief and nudge me along in confidence to get through what is now new. Father, thank You for Your right hand!

Take Action: Dare to place your pain into the right hand of Daddy God. Concentrate on trusting Daddy God, with an innocent, childlike mindset, as He carries you through your spiritual journey.

||||||||||||||||||||||||||||||||||||||||||||||||||||||||||||||||||||||||||||||||||||||||||||||||||||||

Psalms 40:2 He lifted me out of the slimy pit, out of the mud and mire; he set my feet on a rock and gave me a firm place to stand.

||||||||||||||||||||||||||||||||||||||||||||||||||||||||||||||||||||||||||||||||||||||||||||||||||||||

NOTES:

_____

_____

_____

_____

_____

_____

_____

Day 8

I am someone who has fashioned the last twenty years of my life in being a strong person. Yet the vulnerability needed for this healing process, has required me to relinquish my strength. Be that as it may, I must tell you vulnerability has been extremely uncomfortable for me.

You see, the only time I have freely cast aside my strength and clothed in vulnerability was for the one man in my adult life who earned it, my darling husband. Now, ironically in his absence I have too as well.

How ironic that the one man in my adult life that I learned to be vulnerable with is now gone and because of losing him, I am more vulnerable than I have ever been in my entire life.

There are no defenses to withstand grief. Grief can be subtle, loud, rush in fast, lull you slow. Grief can be covert, making you believe it's moved on, only to jump from behind the preverbal bush and gut punch you. **At times, all you can do is take the hit and allow it to have its way.** In the early stages of this new life adjustment, I have learned that allowing grief to do what it is going to do, has given me a better strategy towards healing. I haven't given up, quit or surrendered to sulking, I have just stopped trying to predict the healing timeline. Allowing myself to feel it, feel all of it, so I can determine my next move. That is where my strength is today. **There is strength in vulnerability.**

There are days when the thoughts of how great of a loss this was, wants to consume me. It is in those moments when I must be able to identify the danger of going down that path, so I may pivot.

I'll give you an example, maybe it's more of a confession. I've had thoughts of other couples, and because I know a little bit about those relationships, I've thought, how could THEIR husbands' lives be spared, and my husband be taken? You must be clutching your pearls to know my contemptable thoughts, but I'm being honest. I don't say it aloud, but I have thought it, and thinking it is the same as saying it. Thoughts like these are counter-productive to healing. When we allow the thoughts of the flesh to have life, they will rule over us and before you know it, kill your spirit. It's in those dark and unmentionable moments, that we must be determined to be led by the Holy Spirit which dwells within. Commit to being honest with yourself and to recognize thoughts like these that indicate the need for spiritual CPR.

Take action: How can you be more vulnerable to the leading of the Holy Spirit? What thoughts have tried to rob you of your peace and joy? Work to intentionally activate the peace you have in Christ Jesus.

||||||||||||||||||||||||||||||||||||||||||||||||||||||||||||||||||||||||||||||||||||||||||||||

Col 3:2, Set your minds on things above, not on earthly things

||||||||||||||||||||||||||||||||||||||||||||||||||||||||||||||||||||||||||||||||||||||||||||||

NOTES:

_____

_____

_____

_____

Day 9

Have you ever opened a cabinet, or a drawer and things began to fall out? That's the worst, right? If that has happened to you, then it is likely that you weren't very careful at how you placed the items inside. Perhaps you were in a rush, or the entire drawer had to be re-organized, and you didn't feel like it at the time or maybe you just didn't notice how you placed the items inside. I've experienced this a time or two.

Just like the mismanaged drawer, we have to pay attention to the state of our hearts during any transition in our lives. If we allow corrupt things to seep in, corrupt things will spill out. Do not get consumed with fluctuating emotions, memories, losses, negative encounters, or poor thoughts. Your focus is to pay attention to how to protect and strengthen our source of life.

We need to use the Word of God as a ready resource, to penetrate deep into our hearts. Our pursuit of utilizing the Word to heal must be deliberate. It will take, not just effort, but willingness to nurture the Word of life over our lives if we are to successfully undergo a spiritual heart transplant. If we want the primary reason for us to live to be God's will, we can't be in a rush busying ourselves away from the pain. We cannot wait to feel inspired to organize our thoughts or emotions, we have to actively pursue God and the mind of Christ.

Finally, mustn't be careless leaving our hearts open to random media, conversations or elements of darkness. The results of being in a rush, unorganized or naive towards our duty encourages wayward emotions and feelings that will tailspin into grievous landmines. We must discipline our efforts to guard what is so very precious and powerful, our hearts.

Take Action: How can you begin to take back your rightful duty as a guard over your heart?

How will you change your daily routines so that your heart is a priority? What have you let enter in your heart lately that is spilling out into your life and causing a mess? Find a passage of scripture that will aid in a spiritual heart transplant and speak it over your life as needed.

‖‖

Proverbs 4:23 Above all else, guard your heart, for everything you do flows from it.

‖‖

NOTES:

_____

_____

_____

_____

_____

_____

_____

Day 10

Some days, my sorrow takes the front seat - without even asking. When this happens, I experience a secondary emotion of fear, parallel to the road of grief that I have been traveling. It comes most often when I feel I have allowed my grief to delay my God given assignments and responsibilities. I call it "woe layering". It is tough when woe layering happens because it feels like my pit has a pit. Or like I'm straddling two lanes on the road. A road to nowhere. I need not commit to either lane. I need to find the exit. To exit, I have learned to acknowledge how I feel and turn to God for His mercy. It is vital to embrace processing, as part of the healing process If we intend to effectively overcome the obstacles faced. God's grace is extremely kind, and He is not caught off guard by our feelings. On the contrary, we have all been downloaded with various feelings as part of the "welcome to earth" package God included upon our birth arrival. He put those emotions in place to help us identify what we were experiencing and to help us understand when we need help. We are not serving ourselves by ignoring them or feeling guilty for having them. Feelings are here for us to have. They are only risky when we behave as if they are ALL we have. Thankfully, having the perseverance to overcome has been producing something powerful within me that I don't yet understand and frankly I can't quite see yet. I trust God even if I can't quite trace His footprints, He knows the road I am on. He is in the midst, nudging me to pursue my identity in Christ at all costs. When I know who I am, then I know what I am capable of through the One that dwells within me.

Take Action: Ask yourself, what has been the battle in your mind regarding your identity? How can you gain a greater understanding of who you are in Christ, to gain the victory in your current situation? Write down three key scriptures that you can speak over your thoughts daily when the wrong identity tries to creep in.

||||||||||||||||||||||||||||||||||||||||||||||||||||||||||||||||||||||||||||||||||||||||||||||||||

Ephesians 1:3 Praise be to the God and Father of our Lord Jesus Christ, who has blessed us in the heavenly realms with every spiritual blessing in Christ

||||||||||||||||||||||||||||||||||||||||||||||||||||||||||||||||||||||||||||||||||||||||||||||||||

NOTES:

_____

_____

_____

_____

_____

_____

_____

Day 11

Today's goal? Organize some of my husband's things to share for donation or keep for myself and family. Overall, I was successful, and I have to say, proud of myself for being able to make progress and keeping my personal commitment to start to resolve his personal belongings. The thing that I found amazing, was the smell of his clothes from the day he passed away. They were still in the hospital bag and still smelling like him.

You must understand, my husband was a fanatic for certain lotions that he lathered (inside joke) onto himself with conviction every morning. In fact, one of the things that stood out to me the most when we were dating was how soft his hands were and how he always smelled so good, for hours :). As soon as I opened the bag, I could smell him like he was standing next to me. I allowed myself the time to take in the moment, take him in once more. God blessed me with a smell that I prayed would never escape me and I treasured it. This great joy I had, stretched my smile ear to ear as I whispered "baby, I miss you so much". The very next thing that I did was fall to my knees and begin to worship my Lord.

In the same way the smell of my husband brought me joy, I want to break open my alabaster box and pour out the oil of my worship daily to bring God joy. I want the fragrance to rise to the heavens. My strong desire is to allow the fragrance of the Holy Spirit to fill this temple (my heart) and that's where I will find my internal peace and eternal joy. I was overwhelmed with the need to get on my knees and let

ABBA know, that I need him and that I am nothing without him, that my gratefulness was full and fresh. The smell of my husband was a good trigger today. We all have triggers that send us to a place, good, bad or indifferent. The hope is that we can always be mindful of what we are experiencing at that very moment. Mindfulness enables us to process emotions to identify what we need for our healing and peace. Be still in your thoughts and tune into God. Trust Him and be still. Your needs are well known to Him.

Take Action: Within your current circumstances, what triggers you to worship God? Do you have an action plan to redirect bad triggers? How can you intentionally be still? What can you do to be more mindful about the sovereignty of God?

Mark 14:3 While he was in Bethany, reclining at the table in the home of Simon the Leper, a woman came with an alabaster jar of very expensive perfume, made of pure nard. She broke the jar and poured the perfume on his head.

NOTES:

_____

_____

_____

_____

_____

_____

Day 12

If you've ever been married, then you can understand me when I say that there is nothing sweeter than the conversations that you have with your spouse. There is a certain intimacy that happens between two individuals that have let their guards down and that have allowed agape love to lead their marriage. Early morning "pillow talk", car convos, over dinner dialogue, inside jokes, finishing each other sentences, non-verbal conversation and cues and even the disagreements; it's all a beautiful thing. Oh, how I miss that! It's hard to go home some days once I remember that he won't be there. Once I remember that the sound of his loud and exciting greeting will not meet me at the door, I get sad. It's a heavy sadness that I just want to stop. During some rides home, the number of tears that come out of my eyes is unbelievable. If I could have anything, I would want to have just one more of our conversations.

Tonight, I choose to write about my feelings because it's very therapeutic and one day someone will read this, and it will help them to know they are not alone. So, what is a God-fearing, praying, fasting, worshiping, girl supposed to do when these feelings come rushing in? I let it happen. I don't fight it. I don't lose hope. I pray. I scream. I focus my breathing. I give myself permission to grieve and surrender myself to God, because I know with all certainty that God is on my side watching over me. That, I never have to question and because I know that that is enough.

God is the lover of your soul, and He is healing you every step of the way.

Take Action: How can you focus more on the bigger picture of God's protection and provision? What do you need to do to trust God more with your feelings? Are there man-made thoughts consuming you about how you should process your feelings? If yes, what do you need to do to cancel those thoughts and adopt the thoughts of your God?

‖‖‖

2 Corinthians 10:5 We demolish arguments and every pretension that sets itself up against the knowledge of God, and we take captive every thought to make it obedient to Christ.

‖‖‖

NOTES:

_____

_____

_____

_____

_____

_____

_____

Day 13

The incredible spiritual gift of rest is available to all who seek it and ask for it. It goes beyond the physical act of getting rest and provides such a great sense of peace. At any given moment, circumstance can give us a heavy load. I love that we can give that load to Jesus. We don't have to carry it, strap it on our backs, wheel it down the street nor does it have to weigh us down. He makes the load easy and light. Give your heaviness to the one that can carry it. Not only does He know what to do with it, He wants you to trust Him with it. The rest that He gives is a supernatural endowment of more faith, more trust, and more peace, for whatever moment that you are in.

Think back on an authority figure from your childhood. If there was something too heavy for you to lift or for you to carry, you would hand it over to them with all the confidence in the world that they could handle it. The confidence you had in their abilities was a direct result of what you had seen them do before. Many times, you witnessed them handle heavy things, things bigger than you. It was a relief for you to hand over the heaviness. In fact you actually expected them to take the weight off your hands. Even as a child there was rest in that moment. Now think about the Lord...hasn't He given you evidence of what He can handle? It makes no sense for us to pull, tug and struggle with the weight. Every battle, every weight, belongs to Jesus, even the battle of grief, loss, pain, anger, sickness and/or bitterness. Give it to him and unwrap the spiritual gift of rest.

We delay healing and often fall deeper into pain when we try to depend on our own strength. We are not required to figure things out on our own. It is a trick of the enemy and deception of our flesh to believe we have to face life's obstacles unassisted. The enemy looks for subtle (and not so subtle) ways to eliminate God in our lives. If we are not careful, we could fall for the enemy's agenda by doing things without the Lord. Remember, as a Kingdom citizen we have a right to Kingdom rest, but it takes living by Kingdom principles and activating the access we have to the King. Let's not confuse thinking about it with praying about it. Prayer is our access.

Take Action: What have you been carrying that is too heavy for you? If you are not sure, ask yourself: what has been causing unrest in your life? Or keeping you up at night? Write down the heaviness and concerns and turn them over to God in prayer, even if it is repetitive.

||||||||||||||||||||||||||||||||||||||||||||||||||||||||||||||||||||||||||||||||||||||||||||||||||||

> **Matthew 11:28-30 "Come to me, all you who are weary and burdened, and I will give you rest. 29 Take my yoke upon you and learn from me, for I am gentle and humble in heart, and you will find rest for your souls. 30 For my yoke is easy and my burden is light."**

||||||||||||||||||||||||||||||||||||||||||||||||||||||||||||||||||||||||||||||||||||||||||||||||||||

NOTES:

_____

_____

_____

_____

_____

Day 14

Over the last week or so, my conversations with God have been quite interesting. Interesting in the sense, that I have repeatedly expressed that I don't want to be controlled by my emotions nor do I want grief to rule my life. Instead of declaring that God is in control and through Him, I have control, I sheepishly hoped grief and emotion away. Which ultimately is giving up control and counterintuitive. After a few of these conversations, the Holy Spirit reminded me the only way to gain this sort of relief is to set my mind on things above. To command every part of my day and to stop using language like: "my grief", "my loss", or "my emotions are out of control". In doing that I have partnered with the negative. Linking arm to arm with sorrow. Yes, I am grieving, and my grief is valid, but grief does not identify me. Loss is not my portion. The emotions I have, are to be felt, but have a maturation date. Hear me, I am not saying those things don't have their place, I am saying don't make them an Idol. When we succumb and yield access only God should have in our lives, it could seem we are worshipping our grief.

Grief has its place, but so does God, we must pull down anything that exalts itself above the knowledge of God and develop a mindset, where my thoughts are now my words. Quickly, audibly, and now faithfully, I speak the word of God and all that He has promised over my life and the circumstances that may arise. But friend, in order to speak the word, we must know the word. Find a passage and speak boldly to take your power back. Rest in the relief of hearing God's words being spoken from our mouths. Even if you feel like the weakest person on planet earth. Speak God's word over and repeatedly until you believe it. This has helped me tremendously and I am so very thankful for the revelation and more importantly that I have the ear to hear.

It is also critically important during your healing process to not isolate yourself from hearing God's word corporately. If you have not been then I urge you to attend a bible teaching church, safely in-person, so that you can hear the unadulterated word of God being spoken. Testimonies of others will encourage you. Corporate worship will uplift you. Simply receiving a kind salutation from a fellow believer will warm your heart. Don't allow the enemy to deceive you into thinking that your refuge is found in isolation. That is a pit of despair that is impossible to climb out of if you allow yourself to be in it for too long.

Take Action: Speak the Word of life in moments where you feel you are losing control. Determine within yourself to build this spiritual muscle and to allow the Holy Spirit to comfort you. When you pray, listening is just as important as speaking. If anything negative enters your thoughts whether subtle or obvious, take control immediately by speaking God's truth

What other overcomers do you know that you can connect with? How do you fight the spirit of isolation? What is the difference between isolation and separation? There is a difference.

||||||||||||||||||||||||||||||||||||||||||||||||||||||||||||||||||||||||||||||||||||||||||||||||||||||||

Romans 10:17 Consequently, faith comes from hearing the message, and the message is heard through the word about Christ.

||||||||||||||||||||||||||||||||||||||||||||||||||||||||||||||||||||||||||||||||||||||||||||||||||||||||

NOTES:

_____

_____

_____

_____

_____

_____

_____

_____

Day 15

Reading his autopsy report this past weekend caused all my emotions to rush in like a tsunami. The natural way I care for him if he is not feeling well kicked in. As if he were still here. I wondered if he understood what he was feeling as the blood clot began to prevent blood flow to his heart. I shifted gears from crying to laughing because this man was convinced that fresh air and water was the cure for everything, which is likely why he asked for water and took a step outside. As I read the report, the movie reel in my mind replayed the day, the moment, the scene. I took for granted the meaning of missing someone. It is more complex than a four-letter word (MISS), one minute I miss him as a whole, the next I miss different parts of him. It can be day to day, moment to moment, minute to minute, but his presence has been replaced with his absence. Being married/one with someone, now being one as an individual. It's hard to put into words, but I can say that it leaves a hole. I feel like there is a hole in my living room floor and I have to just keep walking around it. At night the hole follows me upstairs and invades my space in the bedroom. It's quiet but I know it is there. I have to avoid falling into it, when I get up in the middle of the night to go to the bathroom. It's just always there. I can't fill it with anything or cover it up. I'm just adjusting and learning how to live with it. From learning to wife, to learning to widow, what a hell of a learning curve.

As in past devotional moments, I confess my feelings to the Lord quickly. Verbalizing the very thing that I was missing at the moment and then invited God in to fill that void for me. The great thing about it is that I know that He will. My hope is in Him. He is my anchor and I choose daily to remind myself that he wants me to depend on Him so that He can perform His work in and through me and be glorified. We all have what I call the overcomers anointing but I realize that I've identified it and accepted it and it's the secret ingredient to living a victorious life. People look at me and tell me that I am so strong, and my reply is, no not on my own, it's the strength of God working in me. The overcomer's formula is resilience plus Godly perspective. These two things combined are like a lethal weapon of mass destruction against the enemies' tactics and schemes. It will always add up to victory. So, when this gaping hole that is now a part of my journey wants to take the spotlight and upstage God, I acknowledge it but then I recover quickly from the feeling that I am having and then I ask myself what God says about the way that I am feeling. His word is stored away for those valley moments of despair, when my soul is hungry, and my spirit is thirsty. I find peace in His word and when I speak His words, they send out an S.O.S. to my rescue. His words then find me and pull me through. God is the God that comes through. He's the same God that has come through before and He will come through this time as well. I am confident that my rescue squad is always on call and actually already on the way to my location. They can find me anywhere. The valley is never too deep, wide, or low, but His love is the perfect breadth, length, depth and height for every situation and circumstance. Even this. And at the end of the day, we will overcome, and God will be glorified. He is just good like that. So, be encouraged and strengthened in your weakness. Praise God for his consistency. Be grateful that He isn't fickle like us. Aren't you grateful that He is not led by His emotions like us and aren't you so grateful that He is not sitting around waiting to be inspired before He moves? He moves on our behalf because He loves us, and He cares.

P.s. that hole is getting smaller and smaller

Take Action: Write down three areas of your life that you need healing in. Ask someone to be your prayer partner about these things. I also suggested meditating on these prayers while fasting (consult your doctor first). Journal your progress.

||||||||||||||||||||||||||||||||||||||||||||||||||||||||||||||||||||||||||||||||||||||||||||||||||||||||||||

Ephesians 3:16-18 16 I pray that out of his glorious riches he may strengthen you with power through his Spirit in your inner being, 17 so that Christ may dwell in your hearts through faith. And I pray that you, being rooted and established in love, 18 may have power, together with all the Lord's holy people, to grasp how wide and long and high and deep is the love of Christ

||||||||||||||||||||||||||||||||||||||||||||||||||||||||||||||||||||||||||||||||||||||||||||||||||||||||||||

NOTES:

_____

_____

_____

_____

_____

_____

_____

Day 16

Lonely places are a place for prayer. What I know about Jesus is that he often retreated to secluded places to pray. In our healing processes we have to focus on the fact that we are not alone, and loneliness is a feeling that will pass. It is also important for us to have the right perspective about being separated and in obscurity. We can find so many stories in the bible of individuals that were seemingly alone but were never forsaken because God works behind the scenes. Even when He seems invisible, He's working. Even when He seems quiet, He's speaking. There is never a second of the day that you are not on God's mind.

What I've learned about those times of obscurity is that He is always working things out for the good. Preparing us for what He has prepared for us. Preparation can be lonely because it is personal. If you're in that space now, relish it and be steady in your faith while you wait. Your behaviors in the waiting room are a testimony to how much you trust Him and His perfect plan. The best thing that you can do while you wait is to let go of the tight grip. Stop trying to control the outcome. That is not our job.

Take Action: What two things will you do while you wait? What element of your process are you trying to control? How do you think your need for control started? How has trying to control outcomes served you well?

||||||||||||||||||||||||||||||||||||||||||||||||||||||||||||||||||||||||||||||||||||||||||||||||||||||||||

**Psalms 46:10 He says, "Be still, and know
that I am God; I will be exalted among the
nations, I will be exalted in the earth."**

||||||||||||||||||||||||||||||||||||||||||||||||||||||||||||||||||||||||||||||||||||||||||||||||||||||||||

NOTES:

_____

_____

_____

_____

_____

_____

_____

Day 17

Jealousy... On occasion, I have caught myself looking at other couples with envy and jealousy. Longing for what was once my normal. I miss my husband so much and I often wish I could hold his face in the palm of my hand or watch him walk around the car and open the door for me, or smile at me as he nonverbally nodded my way for an inside joke. Even just resting his hand in the small of my back as he would lead me to a seat. Those things, they sound small until you no longer have them. I felt the unnatural feeling of envy just watching a husband prioritize his wife. I don't want what they have, I just miss what I had. Jealousy doesn't feel like a natural response to me and so then those thoughts are followed with guilt. Guilty because I know those thoughts are not of God. I shared with God that I want to celebrate other couples and pray for them like I previously did before I lost my husband. I told Him that without His help, I was unable to find my way to that space. I knew that God could give me the remedy. Later on, that day, I heard in my heart that every time envy or jealousy rears up, begin to thank God for all the beautiful memories that my husband and I made. I will thank God for every time we held hands so naturally like there were magnets, pulling us together. I'll bless God for every time Antwain wrapped his big arm around my shoulders and I melted into his chest. I'll give God a hallelujah for every time my husband would try and break a bear hug, but I would hold on for a few moments longer and then we would both laugh. Gratitude is a game changer!

Take Action: What self-loathing game do you need to change? How can you be more honest with yourself and with God and then name your issue? Are you stuck in pity city or the valley of despair? Make a list of your woes and then a list of what you are thankful for. I bet I know what list is greater. Give thanks.

1 Thessalonians 5:16-18 Rejoice always, 17 pray continually, 18 give thanks in all circumstances; for this is God's will for you in Christ Jesus.

NOTES:

_____

_____

_____

_____

_____

_____

_____

Day 18

Healing is an intimate personal process and requires very deliberate actions. It is my prayer that I use all of my energy wisely. I know for sure that when I consult with God and make Him my priority that nothing will be taken away from me. My reward will be great and plentiful. Sometimes pain will cause us to run in circles looking for some way to occupy our time so that we can ignore the depth of its sting. Don't prolong the healing process by ignoring pain. We have to have a desire for our hearts and our minds and spirits to be made over and transformed so that our emotions and thoughts won't consume us. I grieve yet knowing that I am not alone and that I am not forsaken is such a beautiful truth that keeps my hope burning. I understand more and more every day that the Lord's attention span is infinite and that He will never ignore me. He never takes his eye off of me. Not only am I loved by Him, I accept His love daily, in order to fulfill His promises for my life.

He desires I be made whole, and I refuse to settle for anything less. I believe in my heart that it is my right and privilege as an heir to have liberty in every area of my life.

I pray that this is resonating with you because healing and wholeness is also your portion. It is not unique to just a few people. God wants this for all of His children. Embrace the pruning and the molding. Some of it may sting, but the sting will assist in your transformation. Additionally, when we hold on tight to God and decide that we won't let go until He blesses us, we can be a blessing to those that we are called to.

Take Action: What actions and goals have you set for yourself and determined to partner with God to be healed? How can you hold yourself accountable for these goals and actions? What area of your life do you need the liberty of Jesus to consume?

‖‖

John 15:1-2 "I am the true vine, and my Father is the gardener. 2 He cuts off every branch in me that bears no fruit, while every branch that does bear fruit he prunes[a] so that it will be even more fruitful.

‖‖

NOTES:

_____

_____

_____

_____

_____

_____

_____

_____

Day 19

This morning I awoke and opened my eyes and tears began to fall. It's been a while since I woke up with the heaviness weighing on me like that. I sat up and wept and expressed my most sorrowful and frustrating thoughts in prayer. About 15 minutes into my prayer of anguish and weeping, my phone rang. I was pressed in my spirit to answer so I did without any guilt of breaking my time in intimate prayer.

I wept to the person on the other line, and she immediately gave me Godly counsel that lifted the burden from my shoulders. I felt the release. It was an immediate answer to my prayers. I was wowed by God AGAIN! These are the types of encounters available to us through complete surrender and by making your heart available for molding and shaping. There are a series of wonders attached to our wonderful counselor that He wants to make available to us as we express total dependency on Him and allow Him to do the work. We don't have to force it and we don't have to beg for it. It's handed to us out of His abundant love for us.

Prayer: God, I desire for my heart and my mind to be pliable to You. Show me how to submit and surrender my heart to You totally, so that I can encounter the liberties of Your grace daily. Thank you for being a God Who is always available and for being One Who has given me access to sweet rest in You. I want to seek You more. I want to learn to wait on You and to give You all of me. I declare today that Your love has lifted me and removed every burden from my shoulders. The heaviness is depleted. In Jesus' name, Amen.

Take Action: List three things in your personal life that are weighing heavy on you. Have you given these things to God in its entirety? My guess is no. Here's how you start, confess these situations to him daily with pure honesty. Get to the root of what is ailing you. For example, if you are upset and hurt and feel like a friend has left you hanging, you may have abandonment issues and your feelings toward this friend are just the fruit of the root of abandonment. You should be confessing abandonment details to God. If you don't know what the root is then seek God for answers and be in the right posture to hear the answer and be ready to take action and do the work for your healing.

||||||||||||||||||||||||||||||||||||||||||||||||||||||||||||||||||||||||||||||||||||||||||||||||||||||||||||||

James 4:7 Submit yourselves, then, to God.
Resist the devil, and he will flee from you.

||||||||||||||||||||||||||||||||||||||||||||||||||||||||||||||||||||||||||||||||||||||||||||||||||||||||||||||

NOTES:

_____

_____

_____

_____

_____

_____

_____

_____

Day 20

The progression of healing through grief, sorrow, anger, loss, etc., will reveal some really interesting behaviors from loved ones, friends and people who say that they love you.

This has been the case throughout my personal experience. I certainly understand and realize that not everyone knows what to say to a person working towards healing.

It's tough because there are no right words, and everyone's process is different. While I would like to believe that everyone has good intentions, some of what people in and around my life have expressed, resulted in poor behaviors and conversations. Make no mistake if you are experiencing this, it is really more about the areas of their life where they need refinement, and not about your own healing.

I found, to successfully brave these unwelcomed storms of "attempted meaningful acts", it is important to identify right away what is taking place. These encounters with others can be blatantly hurtful, inconsiderate, offensive, or even cruel. One encounter left me feeling a sting in my body, as if I had been slapped across the face. It's in those moments that, I pause. Check internally with the Holy Spirit to make sure I am not misinterpreting the moment. Then I follow by immediately asking God that He forgive them, for they know not what they do. I am sharing this because, we have to also agree with the Lord and put the offense to rest. We must consciously decide quickly not to allow; un-forgiveness, bitterness, or offense, to take space or residence in our lives.

Full disclosure, each instance that I chose to be Christ-like instead of tapping into my arsenal of word wounding phrases, was difficult. Remember friends, serving Christ means killing our flesh. This is not only a daily act, but a necessary means for the healing process to take effect.

I heard you... so what do you do when it is not easy to forgive? For me, I ask myself the question, is it worth it? Is it worth my peace? Is it worth me losing rest? What is more important? Being mad or guarding my heart? We must make a decision to protect the one thing from which the issues of life flow. More importantly, our heart is the place where God wants to reside. We need to make room for Him daily. Do not allow seeds of bitterness to gain any depth. The deeper they go, they run the risk of taking root. And roots are harder to remove. Allow no sin or evil to dwell in your tent.

Take Action: Who do you need to forgive on this journey of healing? How has un-forgiveness taken root and showed up in your life? Can you have the courage to give up your right to hold on to the hurt? What anger is festering in you? Pray for those that have hurt you. Ask God and yourself to forgive.

||||||||||||||||||||||||||||||||||||||||||||||||||||||||||||||||||||||||||||||||||||||||||||||||||||

James 1:19-21 My dear brothers and sisters, take note of this: Everyone should be quick to listen, slow to speak and slow to become angry, 20 because human anger does not produce the righteousness that God desires. 21 Therefore, get rid of all moral filth and the evil that is so prevalent and humbly accept the word planted in you, which can save you.

||||||||||||||||||||||||||||||||||||||||||||||||||||||||||||||||||||||||||||||||||||||||||||||||||||

NOTES:

_____

_____

_____

_____

_____

_____

_____

Day 21

Effective listening is such an important element of personal and spiritual development. We have to listen to our bodies to know when something is wrong or when we are lacking something. It is critical in communication and relationships. Effective listening is a skill that we must acquire. Think on this, we listen to our doctors' instructions. At work we listen to the trainer or person who is skilled to orient us to our role. Then it makes sense to listen to the greatest teacher of them all, the Holy Spirit. I am learning that quality time, absorbing information from the Holy Spirit has been the most advantageous for me. It is in those spiritual lessons, where I find my refuge and strength. I don't always know what's taking place at the time, but eventually I feel the peace, or I eventually fall into the depth of the encounter when nothing else is relevant. I even lose awareness in my breathing pattern because there is a beautiful exchange taking place. We give God our attention. He then gives us His easiness and lightness, also known as His grace and mercy.

I can tell you from experience that God is always speaking. Ask yourself are you always listening? May I suggest that when God speaks, don't overthink, or complicate what you hear. To help with your discernment, an easy red flag to discern God's voice vs another is, you shouldn't feel confused at what you hear. God is not a God of confusion. His voice you can trust. Personally, I purpose to allow God's Spirit to control my mind and my desire. This helps my daily mission and points me to the very best decisions I can make. Living in deep dependence on God affords me peace in tumultuous times, Make the life changing decision today to come to God with an open heart and mind and invite him to control your thoughts and plant his desires into your spirit. Build the self-control and the self-discipline necessary to be still and allow him to minister to my heart in the silence.

Take Action: What can you do to spend more time in silent communication with God? How can you change the patterns of your prayers to include more listening? If you are not an effective listener, how has that impacted your communication skills and relationships?

Proverbs 1:5 Let the wise hear and increase in learning, and the one who understands obtain guidance,

NOTES:

_____

_____

_____

_____

_____

_____

_____

Day 22

Today I am so ever grateful for the consistent message of love and light that I receive from the Lord. God is teaching me to live peacefully in Him. Surrounded by His love and void of the guilt and shame related to insecurity. His grace feels like an embrace and because He knows how much I love a good hug; I know it's intentional. In that moment I forget about everything else but His divine comfort. Now I am not suggesting that grace is an individual event. On the contrary, it is a continuum of free-flowing love. Like a fresh shower of manna raining down Releasing the protection, provision, joy, and rest needed to feel loved. It's special. It's personal. I liken it to a big wet snowflake gently landing on your face. Snowflakes are not replicated and melt directly onto your skin upon contact, meaning it's just for you. God has a way of making our intimate moments "just for us" something another may not understand or appreciate. Unique to you. This is what makes His grace a place of trust. A vehicle that He drives. My friends, God invites you to sit in His grace as He moves you through the tough times. The times when your hand to the wheel won't do. He longs to navigate you through these healing stages. I can trust God to bring me through and to bring me over. Perhaps, you like I, are still going through. However, I am learning to sit in the passenger seat as God the Father drives me through the transformation that is taking place. He performs a daily refreshing of my spirit, renewal of my mind, and restoration of hope. Weaving it all together, the perfect tune from a sweet love song He performs as we take the drive. Thank you, Jesus, for the melody.

God speaks our language, and he teaches us his. He meets us right where we are. I encourage you to be more conscious of how grace is showing up in your life daily and even moment by moment.

Take Action: How has the process of healing been transformational for you? How have your thought patterns changed? What can you share with others to encourage them on their journey? What are you learning about yourself? Are you willing to trust God to drive you through?

||||||||||||||||||||||||||||||||||||||||||||||||||||||||||||||||||||||||||||||||||||||||||||||||||||

> **2 Corinthians 12:9 But he said to me, "My grace is sufficient for you, for my power is made perfect in weakness." Therefore I will boast all the more gladly of my weaknesses, so that the power of Christ may rest upon me.**

||||||||||||||||||||||||||||||||||||||||||||||||||||||||||||||||||||||||||||||||||||||||||||||||||||

NOTES:

_____

_____

_____

_____

_____

_____

_____

_____

Day 23

As my husband's birthday approached, I could feel the anxiety and the fear of the unexpected enter into my thoughts and my soul. I didn't know how I was going to feel on that day, knowing how very special we made birthdays for one another. I mentioned earlier that he and I shared so many firsts together and how now I have to experience a lot of new firsts without him - too many to number. The frustration of not knowing what to expect has the potential to control me in every way. I must count on God to show up like He always does.

His track record of keeping me in times of unexpected situations is flawless, when I turn to Him. I hope to remind you, as well as remind myself to turn to Him. We are not required to do this alone. God lifts the heavy things; we lift our requests.

Then I thought of God's history with me and realized, the Holy Spirit has comforted me through so many special dates and events already, his birthday will be no different. There is no difficulty that the Holy Spirit is ill-equipped for. We only need to patiently wait on the Lord. Our impatience to figure things out or to have a plan in place, creates the anxiety and the fear that wants to rule us. When we wait on the Lord for answers we receive renewed strength, a resurgence of hope and a new awareness of His continual presence. God's omniscience within all of our daily routines, and within every area of our healing is the secret sauce that satisfies the depth of our spirits. It's all we need.

Take Action: What answers, strategies or plans are you trying to figure out on your own? Are there dates or holidays that you have in mind that may bring up uneasy feelings or unrest? Give it to God, take it one day at a time. Be in no rush for that day to be over.

||||||||||||||||||||||||||||||||||||||||||||||||||||||||||||||||||||||||||||||||||||||||||||||||||||||

Psalms 27:14 Wait for the Lord; be strong, and let your heart take courage; wait for the Lord!

||||||||||||||||||||||||||||||||||||||||||||||||||||||||||||||||||||||||||||||||||||||||||||||||||||||

NOTES:

_____

_____

_____

_____

_____

_____

_____

_____

Day 24

Having to participate in your healing is a task on its own but having to do it during a global pandemic has presented certain challenges for sure. The isolation associated with living through loss has been tough and difficult to negotiate at times. Now we are introduced a new layer of adjustment.

I must say, I am grateful for how technology has played such an incredible role in keeping us all connected to one another. Getting adjusted to different means of communication was not easy at first but by the instruction of the Holy Spirit, I have realized that it's necessary to be flexible and open to learn new things. God wants to do a new thing in us which means old habits, old ways of thinking and stiff-necked mindsets won't work where He is taking us. Seeking the Lord for a mindset that will align with His plan for us is critical to our healing process.

It is important to constantly check our perspectives regarding our circumstances. We have to challenge ourselves and be sure that we are not allowing external voices and worldviews to dictate how we perceive what we are experiencing. What does God say about it? Let's be mindful of what is influencing our decisions and our behaviors. Old habits and thought patterns keep us stuck and unable to pursue purpose.

Take Action: How many times have you come to a conclusion influenced by the media? What is a thought pattern that you would like to change for good? How can you be more open to learning new things and being more flexible to prepare for where God is taking you?

‖‖‖

Isaiah 43:19 Behold, I am doing a new thing; now it springs forth, do you not perceive it? I will make a way in the wilderness and rivers in the desert.

‖‖‖

NOTES:

_____

_____

_____

_____

_____

_____

_____

Day 25

Let's continue to talk about patterns and habits. What does your morning routine look like? People that win in life don't become successful overnight. Daily routines are foundational for setting them up to win. Sure, I could choose to sulk every morning and to allow my feelings to get the best of me. I could also choose to sleep into the very last minute and so could you but how would that prepare us for a day of victorious living? Newsflash… it won't. Our morning habits and patterns require self-discipline, there is no way around it. One of my favorite motivating quotes goes like this; "discipline is the difference between what you want now and what you want most." Friends, decide what you want most and commit. God can do all things, but we must do our part. We should be committing to laying the foundation and setting the tone toward healing. It takes fortitude and determination to fight past your feelings and to push into the presence of the Lord. But we must.

If you start your day with prayer, pray without ceasing throughout the day and finish your day in prayer, you have created a recipe for success. In your prayers seek and listen with intent for wisdom. Discern what your soul requires and how to make it happen. Receive the supernatural strength to plan your mornings according to the will of God.

Take Action: Implement a plan to make mornings be more productive. Set yourself up for victorious living. What patterns or habits of prayer do you need to adjust or improve to help you to remain in God's will?

||||||||||||||||||||||||||||||||||||||||||||||||||||||||||||||||||||||||||||||||||||||||||||||||||||

Psalms 90:14 Satisfy us in the morning with your steadfast love, that we may rejoice and be glad all our days.

||||||||||||||||||||||||||||||||||||||||||||||||||||||||||||||||||||||||||||||||||||||||||||||||||||

NOTES:

_____

_____

_____

_____

_____

_____

_____

Day 26

Being on this journey can feel excruciating at times. I have my days when I want to scream (sometimes I do), kick, throw things, punch a wall in or break some glass to ease the discomfort of the process. Let's face it, it doesn't feel good. I have an entirely new understanding of the meaning of being gracefully broken. I first had to understand grace and then understand brokenness. Grace is freely given to us, and it is in the very essence of Who God is. God is favorably inclined toward us. He only wants what is best for us and He demonstrates this graciousness in everything that He does. My definition of brokenness is the state of being defeated and having to surrender during a difficult time that comes along when things are presumably painless and steady.

Though you may be in the state of being defeated, know, and understand that God's favor is all over you. You may not see how, but you will be a better person in the end. Something good will come out of your pain not because it's all good but because it is all God and He can't fail. Brokenness is an opportunity for a breakthrough. He may not have caused the brokenness, but it has not taken Him by surprise. You can find solace in God's character and in His resume. Has He failed you yet? Your pain will not be in vain. Your surrender is for your benefit. The providential care of our heavenly father is a promise that we can count on. I know some days that it doesn't feel like it, but you will get through this. I believe. Will you also believe?

Take Action: What can you do to learn more about the character of God? What other times in your life has God pulled you through a difficult time? If you don't already have one, start a gratitude journal.

||||||||||||||||||||||||||||||||||||||||||||||||||||||||||||||||||||||||||||||||||||||||||||||||||||

John 1:16 For from his fullness we have all received, grace upon grace.

||||||||||||||||||||||||||||||||||||||||||||||||||||||||||||||||||||||||||||||||||||||||||||||||||||

NOTES:

_____

_____

_____

_____

_____

_____

_____

_____

Day 27

Have you ever found yourself using cavalier language when you speak about your situation? For example, "I don't know how I'll ever get better", or "this is too much for one person to handle". I'm raising my hand over here as I type. I am certainly guilty of letting these types of things slip off of my tongue. It is careless to choose carnal language for a situation that requires supernatural power. We cannot afford to allow lackadaisical words to fall out of our mouths. We have too much on the line. We must grasp an understanding of the power that we have on our tongue. Then use it accordingly. Use it to build ourselves up, to knock the enemy's devices down, to call out to the Lord, to ignite supernatural assistance. To speak truth to power! Why? Not only because, but the devouring enemy is also waiting for our faith to waiver so he can sucker punch us in the gut. But also, when we speak contrary to God's truth about us, it is an indication of a crack in our foundation - our faith. It may seem harmless at the time but how quickly can these phrases become common vernacular and ultimately define the next moment we live in?

The cost of our wholeness was paid in full on the cross, a cost that we can never pay on our own. Jesus paid it all! Let us not minimize His sacrifice by speaking counter-productive to the victory that He has already won for us. I challenge you to be more attentive to your choice of words. When I say challenge, I truly want you to picture me in your face, Kleenex in hand, telling you to dry your tears and change your language. Challenging you to be better to yourself, by placing the power of your words in the right direction. Sometimes we must coach ourselves in the things the Lord has already spoken. It's not corny, it's restorative. Be willing to correct yourself quickly, for example instead of saying "I don't know how I'll ever get better", say that "the Lord is the strength of my heart and my portion forever". Instead of saying "this is too much for one person to handle", say "when I am weak then the Lord is made strong". Speak His Word and bring life to your soul and to your spirit. Everything around you will begin to line up with what you have spoken out of your mouth. Start today. Don't allow negative talking to be in your midst. Shut it down and counter that talk with the awe-inspiring word of God.

Take Action: How many times a day do you think that you allow counterproductive language to spill out of your mouth? I challenge you to take a tally over the next three days. What do you need to do so that the word of God is the first word that comes to mind?

‖‖‖

Proverbs 18:21 Death and life are in the power of the tongue, and those who love it will eat its fruits.

‖‖‖

NOTES:

_____

_____

_____

_____

_____

Day 28

I'll never forget the day that I sought the Lord in prayer for relief from the gut-wrenching emotional pain that I was feeling. I felt the push of the Holy Spirit to take a bike ride. On my ride, I got the opportunity to help someone that was in need medically. When she was better and ready to leave with her husband, I began to weep and to pray with them. I was so grateful to the Lord for answering my prayer. The lesson I learned that day was the principle of helping others when you are in pain. Giving to others, will always take the attention off of you and put the attention on God. In those moments of servanthood, the Lord does for you that you cannot do for yourself behind the scene.

I beg you to make it a part of your healing process to get out of your own way and out of your comfort zone and to help someone else. It can be as minor as driving someone to the grocery store every week. Whatever you do, do it as unto the Lord and watch God work. What happens in sacrificial serving is supernatural no doubt. It will change your perspective and it will bring you joy, the kind of joy that you don't get from people, places, or things.

Take Action: When was the last time that you selflessly served someone else? How can you make this principle a regular part of your life? How does serving others get you outside of your comfort zone and into God's purpose for that moment?

||||||||||||||||||||||||||||||||||||||||||||||||||||||||||||||||||||||||||||||||||||||||||||||||||||||||||||

Matthew 20:28 even as the Son of Man came not to be served but to serve, and to give his life as a ransom for many."

||||||||||||||||||||||||||||||||||||||||||||||||||||||||||||||||||||||||||||||||||||||||||||||||||||||||||||

NOTES:

_____

_____

_____

_____

_____

_____

_____

Day 29

Beep, beep, beep goes the sound to warn us that there is a vehicle moving close to us. That sound alerts us to prepare as we decide to take action. Triggers to our pain, sorrow and grief don't necessarily give a warning sign. I wish they did. I was triggered today by something I was asked, and this feeling of sorrow came rushing over me. I never saw it coming, there was no beep to help identify the shift. It was a whirlwind of emotions that came in 2.5 seconds. Suddenly, in the very same minute, the Lord brought something to my mind to make me laugh. I experienced receiving joy for sorrow in real time. It was incredible! God is amazing at how He is the mastermind behind our healing process. The relief that the laughter provided me was a beautiful reminder that Jesus was totally God and totally human at the same time. He was assigned the ultimate sacrifice so that we would never feel alone and that we would know that He knows, how we feel. When the agonizing cross we've had to bear becomes too great, it is easy to feel like our problem is unique, or that no one understands how we are feeling. In those moments, I think of how Jesus must have felt in His human form. How tragic, to be tortured by the people He was giving His all for? The loneliness of only having a few of his followers continue on the path with Him to the place, where on the cross He hung? What did it feel like for Him to still be saving others as His life was fleeting? Then the weight of my cross pales in comparison, and often my sorrow turns to praise.

Take Action: In what ways can you begin to practice seeing the Godly perspective in your current situation? Have you literally asked God to replace your primary emotion with His primary plan for you? Ask, Lord, replace this sadness with laughter.

||||||||||||||||||||||||||||||||||||||||||||||||||||||||||||||||||||||||||||||||||||||||||||

Isaiah 61:3 to grant to those who mourn in Zion—to give them a beautiful headdress instead of ashes, the oil of gladness instead of mourning, the garment of praise instead of a faint spirit; that they may be called oaks of righteousness, the planting of the Lord, that he may be glorified.[c]

||||||||||||||||||||||||||||||||||||||||||||||||||||||||||||||||||||||||||||||||||||||||||||

NOTES:

_____

_____

_____

_____

_____

_____

_____

_____

Day 30

Do you know people in your life that always seem to have joy or peace? What do you think that these people have in common? It is not a special skill or an ability to have joy or peace, it is a mindset. More specifically, a critical thinking mindset. This is a mindset that God intends for us to have as His children.

We know that there is not a shortage of tribulations or hard times in this depleted world. Our feelings have the propensity to get the best of us if we allow them to. But there is good news, we can choose to have joy and peace every day. Careful, when choosing between joy and sorrow, for whichever we choose will flow out of us. A way to remain in a posture of abundant living, even during chaos, is to remain curious about who God is and about who He made you to be. This is a strategy that I personally use to slap myself out of any slump or any moment when my location is, pity city. I'm sure you know the feeling, when the negative wants to rise up and rule your disposition. If we proclaim that Jesus is the Lord of our lives, then we must apply that truth to our thinking and our response to difficult times. Unfortunately, we have been brainwashed by a dark culture that causes us to gravitate and potentially latch onto negative thoughts, offenses, hurt feelings and painful emotions. I am not negating the reality of our feelings, but I appeal to you, that we do not have to allow our feelings to govern us.

I wake up daily with an on-purpose mindset about my day, turning my day over to God and seeking Him for direction. If my mood is off, I acknowledge it, confess it and give God authority over it. See, the enemy wants us to ignore it, stuff it down and not share it with God. He hopes we will leave the house emotionally disturbed and set out to wound others throughout the day. Nope! Unfortunately for the enemy, I don't play with him, I turn him and his tactics over to my father, Abba God. I will not be willingly used to wound or drag someone into a pit. The repercussions of unchecked sorrow can have a lasting impact on relationships and opportunities. That's what the enemy is after, the long-range pain plan. Not just this day, not just me. He wants to use my circumstances destructively every day, toward everyone I touch, and everyone they touch, and so on. With this in mind, I promptly surrender to the Holy Spirit to do something for me that I cannot do for myself. *He leads me and guides me down the path of righteousness for His namesake.* I determine that my thoughts will line up with the path God has for me. I believe what God says about me and I am willing to renounce the familiar spirits that come to distract me from the rights that I have as a Kingdom citizen.

Take Action: Fix your mind on things that are pure and lovely. Use curiosity to discover more about your true identity and the character of God. List what old mindsets are defining who you are. What does it mean for you to be a Kingdom Citizen?

Philippians 4:8 ESV Finally, brothers, whatever is true, whatever is honorable, whatever is just, whatever is pure, whatever is lovely, whatever is commendable, if there is any excellence, if there is anything worthy of praise, think about these things.

NOTES:

_____

_____

_____

_____

_____

_____

_____

_____

Day 31

Where is my future? The sudden loss of a spouse, job, home, and any other entity that provided security, can cause you to also grieve the future plans, aspirations and goals you had. I'm realizing now, although I am certainly still grieving the loss of my husband, I am also grieving the future that I thought I would have with him.

To be totally transparent, I am questioning God about whether or not my discernment meter is off, or if He decided to switch the plans up on me without giving me notice. It hurts to not be able to do things as I planned or expected to do with my loving husband. How do you now recover from this? How do I adjust to this new life without falling deep into a hole of despair or an emotional rut?

Simply put, there have been times when I stood in the grocery store checkout line, baffled as to who is now going to carry my groceries and make me laugh all the way back to the car. "This ain't right Jesus! I need answers" (is my go to line) for moments like this. As I am writing this, I am returning my rental car, (sitting in the return aisle a lot longer then I needed to) pondering the fact that I just successfully had a five-day vacation! ALONE! Wow! This is an accomplishment that I saw to be very far off one-year ago. Back then, the very thought of it then made me cringe. The truth is, if you just continue to trust the Lord with your pain, confusion, questions, unimaginable future and keep pressing forward daily, He will put all of the pieces together. He will direct your path because the puzzle is already finished. AMEN! I continue to practice reminding myself that, the knowledgeable, capable, creative, thoughtful, gracious, loving, trustworthy divine Father is in charge of my future. It is that which carries me through. Knowing who God is at the core of His character is an important factor that will ensure peace when the storms of life get a little foggy or chaotic. Knowing Who Jehovah – He is, will be Jehovah Jireh – The Lord will provide who will also be Jehovah Nissi – the Lord my banner will fight for me is a mental, spiritual, and emotional rescue plan. I believe that I will not lack anything. I believe that I do not have to fight any battles – even the battlefield of my mind. I just need to stand. And even in those lonely days trying to imagine my future moments, I am not alone!

Take Action: Take inventory of the plans you thought would be part of your future but have been interrupted by a life event. Reconcile these changes in your spirit through trusting God. Are you angry with God for the disruption? If yes, confess it and know that what He has planned will prosper you!

> **Proverbs 3:5-6 Trust in the Lord with all your heart and lean not on your own understanding; in all your ways submit to him, and he will make your paths straight.**

Prayer: Lord, help us to see Your very hands shaping and molding our future into Your perfect shape and function. Help us to trust you when things do not go as we have planned and for us to always make You our Plan A. You are our priority and not an option. Give us a hunger and thirst to search Your word for a deeper understanding of Your character, the meaning of Your names, and answers to our struggles. Forgive us for moments of anger and when we may even try to push You away. And we thank you that we can never hide from You and that there is not anywhere that we will go that You will not be. Thank You for Your grace. In Jesus' name, Amen.

NOTES:

_____

_____

_____

_____

_____

_____

_____

_____

Bonus Day 32

"Whatchew talking bout Willis?" Have you ever received a prophetic word about your situation which is just confirmation of what the Lord has already told you? You find yourself desperately seeking God for clarity?

Clarity because, you weren't expecting to get confirmation on what had God originally said so quickly? Oh, just me? Okay. Well, that happened to me recently. I received it. The giver of the word and I shared tears. We went our separate ways and I spent about ten days just revisiting the prophetic word and saying "wow"! That was really all that I could say about it because it was so clear and exactly what I needed to hear in that moment. However, I still felt I needed more clarity and understanding. God is faithful and I trust His track record, that because I asked, He will make sure I receive it. Just as the Lord saw fit to give me confirmation of His word, through His chosen vessel, He will see fit to answer me in His timing. As His child, I have the privilege to "ask him to see past the mountains" as my Pastor says. While it is not always easy to wait on the Lord and be of good cheer, it is necessary so that we do not move and act prematurely. When we seek His face, not only will we find what we long for, it will feel like He has added to us. I choose to seek my creator for answers and not look for answers from His creation. I cannot look to people, places or things for revelation or direction. Yet if He chooses to use those listed above to speak to me then so be it. After all, He willingly speaks to us in our language so that we can understand Him fully. Such a beautiful thing. Thank you, Jesus! And just as He seeks to be close to me, I want to always nurture the necessities of my relationship with Him. I want to be like the deer that pants for streams of water. I want my soul to pant for God. Ultimately this is what is happening when you are seeking answers. Your soul is longing to be fulfilled. When we seek Him, He will answer.

Take Action: When was the last time that you asked God the tough questions? Its ok to ask, He is not afraid of your tough questions, you know. I dare you take a shot at it; you will be surprised at the results. Also, while you are seeking God for answers, please do not neglect the practice of responding to instructions without delay.

What have you received confirmation about but have failed to ask for more clarity? What are the emotions that are attached to the hesitancy you have in asking God for answers?

||||||||||||||||||||||||||||||||||||||||||||||||||||||||||||||||||||||||||||||||||||||||

Psalms 42:1 As the deer pants for streams of water, so my soul pants for you, my God.

||||||||||||||||||||||||||||||||||||||||||||||||||||||||||||||||||||||||||||||||||||||||

NOTES:

_____

_____

_____

_____

_____

Conclusion:

Over this past year, I have been reminded of the importance of owning and operating from the spiritual authority that I have through Christ Jesus.

I do not, we do not, have to succumb to or accept the attacks on our lives, destinies, minds, children, finances, ministries etc. We have real supernatural authority and have the legal right to appropriate the blood of Jesus and receive our victory, thus proclaiming the Lord's glory! We must be in continual practice of Christian principles, in order to strengthen, not weaken, the spiritual authority that we have and are entitled to.

The strength and power of our authority is rooted in faith, therefore influenced by our thoughts and actions. If we believe this to be true, then we must be mindful of the breakthroughs that come and intensify as we continue to grow in faith and practice of God's principles. Having a Masterpiece Mindset means that your breakthroughs will be connected to a number of purpose driven principles and practices. For the sake of efficiency, I will focus on nine:

1. The condition of our hearts
2. Our affection toward God
3. Our consistent sharing of the gospel and our testimonies
4. Trust in God

5. How we stand in the face of adversity
6. Increasing our spiritual sight
7. The consistency to serving others
8. Where our hope lies and
9. Digesting the Word of God.

Again, this is not an exhaustive list, but this is a list of what I have practiced inciting true chain breaking in my life. Practicing these principles provides me with immeasurable Godly strength, wisdom, and courage to pursue and to take my rightful place in the Kingdom of God. It is walking out these principles, which keep my emotions in check, when they try to rule me. There is no time to leave room or acceptance for complacency, long-term discouragement, or inactivity toward my faith. The more that I partner with the Holy Spirit, the more I experience, joy, peace and rest. Don't settle for less than what God has intended for your life. Believe that you have been destined for greater works through Jesus and greater you shall have. Remember, this is not a one-time event. This is ongoing.

The time is now for a mindset shift. You are God's handiwork, his Masterpiece. It is time to live like it and to do all the good things that he planned for you a long time ago. The kind of thinking that has gotten you here will not take you to where God desires for you to go.

Take Action: Starting today, what can you eliminate or minimize from your daily practices that are not serving your spirit well? How can you actively and consistently partner with the Holy Spirit for breakthroughs in specific areas in your life? What do you do well that you can do more of? Who do you need to collaborate with to develop what is missing from your spiritual disciplines?

||||||||||||||||||||||||||||||||||||||||||||||||||||||||||||||||||||||||||||||||||||||||||||||||||||

John 14:12 Very truly I tell you, whoever believes in me will do the works I have been doing, and they will do even greater things than these, because I am going to the Father.

||||||||||||||||||||||||||||||||||||||||||||||||||||||||||||||||||||||||||||||||||||||||||||||||||||

CPSIA information can be obtained
at www.ICGtesting.com
Printed in the USA
LVHW081622010422
714846LV00004B/6